CALLING YOU

A Confirmation Course for All Ages

New Edition

SHARON J. SWAIN

MOREHOUSE PUBLISHING
A Continuum imprint
www.morehousepublishing.com

Morehouse
A Continuum imprint
The Tower Building
11 York Road
London SE1 7NX

4775 Linglestown Road
Harrisburg
PA 17112

www.continuumbooks.com
www.morehousegroup.com

First published 1993
Reissued 1994, 1996
This edition 1999
Reprinted 2005

British Library Cataloguing in Publication Data
A catalogue record for this book is available from the British Library

ISBN 0-8192 8142 5

Illustrations by Sister Anna SSM

Typeset by Kenneth Burnley, Wirral, Cheshire.
Printed and bound in Great Britain by Biddles Ltd,
King's Lynn, Norfolk

To the Confirmation Group Leader

Calling You allows you to create your own Confirmation course. Whether this is to last for six weeks or a year, sufficient material is offered for you to tailor an exciting and challenging course for young people or for adults.

Not every suggestion in the book is therefore intended to be used in the Confirmation course – you will need to select and discard ideas to suit your circumstances. Neither are the Units in this book placed in any particular order. Arrange the order to suit yourself and the Confirmation candidates.

Each member of the group will need a copy of *Calling You*, so that they can look at the material marked *On your own* and begin preparation for the next topic. *Research* can be allocated as desired, and *Groupwork* exercises chosen to fit local circumstances. Each Unit also offers a short time of *Closing worship.*

This book aims to stimulate Confirmation candidates through affective education to move a further step on in their Christian journey. Ready-made answers are not offered. *Calling You* assumes that you will have a certain level of Christian knowledge and will be able to learn alongside the members of your group. You are not expected to have all the answers!

Finally it must also be noted that *Calling You* can be used with Christians of any age.

To the Confirmation Candidate

Calling You is a book especially designed for new Christians like yourself to help you learn more about God and about your Christian faith.

Each week there are ideas to try out *On your own* at home, and you will need to find somewhere peaceful then! There are also suggestions for **Research** so that when you attend the Confirmation meeting you will already know something about the topic.

Each topic has some information to help you, but you will really learn more by exploring what it means with others in the group. So your Confirmation course should first and foremost be an *active, doing* course and not just a listening one!

Lastly, don't expect your Confirmation Group Leader to know all the answers, because she or he won't – those who lead groups are also learning about God. As Christians we are all on a journey back to God, and we may not know the answers until we finish the journey!

CORE ELEMENTS OF YOUR CONFIRMATION COURSE

As a group choose which subjects you feel are essential for your Confirmation course from those given below. Obviously these will vary, depending on whether you intend to meet for six weeks or six months. There is no specific order to the Units (one doesn't necessarily lead to the next), so choose the order you prefer and the assignments most suited to your group.

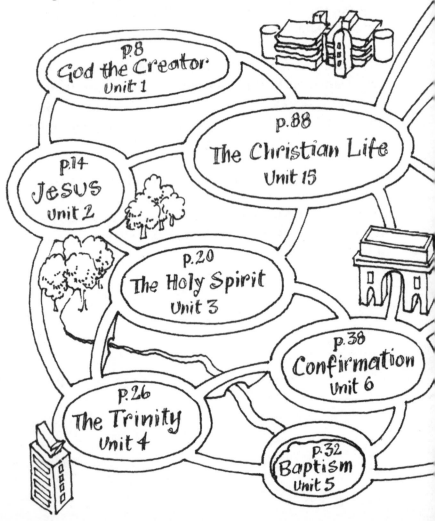

p.8
God the Creator
Unit 1

p.88
The Christian Life
Unit 15

p.14
Jesus
Unit 2

p.20
The Holy Spirit
Unit 3

p.38
Confirmation
Unit 6

p.26
The Trinity
Unit 4

p.32
Baptism
Unit 5

UNIT 1 – GOD THE CREATOR

ON YOUR OWN

Spend some time alone being still. You could play some quiet music in the background, and concentrate on looking at a favourite picture, or a candle flame (if possible), or even a flower.

Let your mind and body become still. Try to ignore any odd thoughts that come into your mind, and just look at the picture, candle or flower. Do this for a few moments until you feel very calm.

 Ask yourself the question:

 Next take a pencil and some paper and try to draw a picture of, or describe, God. What do you think God is like? Use your imagination!

 Finally, end this time on your own by looking up Psalm 66 in the Bible and reading verses 1–4. Here's someone who bubbles over with joy about God!

RESEARCH

Ask two or three people, who are Christians, the following questions:

(a) What do you think God is like? Or, can you describe God?

(b) When you say your prayers what name(s) do you use for God?

There are many different descriptions of God in the Bible. Look up the following verses, and then see how many others you can find. There are many more!

Psalm 104, verse 10 (God as Creator).
Exodus, chapter 15, verse 18 (God as King).
Exodus, chapter 15, verse 6 (God as Warrior).
Psalm 23, verse 1 (God as Shepherd).
Matthew, chapter 6, verse 9 (God as Father).

WITH OTHERS – THINKING IT THROUGH

At Baptism and Confirmation we affirm that we believe in God 'creator of heaven and earth' (see Common Worship Initiation Services). For many people this can be a problem, for they cannot see God, the Creator. Yet we can see what God does in the world and in our own lives – for instance, through the beauty or complexity of the world around us, or the loving-kindness of another human being.

Each one of us experiences God's love and creative power in our lives in a different way from other people. So each one of us will have a different 'picture' of God the Creator.

WITH OTHERS – GROUPWORK

Together with others in the group choose some of the following activities to learn more about God the Creator.

> *In twos discuss the pictures and/or words about God* that you have produced on your own during the week. After a few moments, as a group, brainstorm the words 'God is . . .' on a large piece of paper. Don't reject any words. Then, see if you can come up with a description of God the Creator that all the group can support.

> *Create a tableau* to describe God. In groups of three or four discuss what you have learnt about God *On your own* and through *Research,* and then create a group tableau or 'photograph' of God the Creator.

Read Genesis, chapter 1, then look at the following statements. Do group members agree or disagree with them?

- God is neither male nor female, therefore we shouldn't use 'Father' to describe God.
- God made the world in six days.
- God made the world, and scientists are exploring how this took place.
- God made the world for us to use its resources and throw them away.
- God cares about the world.
- God has forgotten about the world.

Read Psalm 139, verses 1–18, and then allocate each member of the group one or more verses of the Psalm. Have available a large number of photographs and pictures so that each person can choose one to go with their verse(s). Read the whole Psalm again, with each person reading their verse(s) and holding up the pictures as they occur.

Make a collage out of words, pictures and music to tell others about God as Creator. Work as a group where possible. Start by writing a poem about Creation. Accompany this with pictures or a tableau describing God's world; and sing or play suitable music (e.g. 'Father we love you' (*Mission Praise*), 'The earth is the Lord's' (*Mission Praise*), or 'Ubi Caritas' (Taizé)). Arrange to present this as an offering in church.

Go for a walk, in the town or countryside. Simply be silent and look around you. Where is God here? How does God speak to you and those who live here?

CLOSING WORSHIP

Sit in a circle. Place one or more items in the centre on which to focus: perhaps a candle, an icon, or an interesting piece of wood or stone. You might also wish to burn incense or joss sticks.

Read Psalm 134 or John, chapter 3, verses 16–18. Use the Litany below and close by singing 'He's got the whole wide world' or 'The earth is the Lord's' (*Mission Praise*).

Leader: Lord God, you know each one of us and hold us securely in your hand. Keep us close to you. Lord, hear us.

All: Lord, graciously hear us.

Leader: Lord God, you love us as a father or mother loves a child. Help us to remember your love always. Lord, hear us.

All: Lord, graciously hear us.

Leader: Lord God, you protect us with your mighty power when we choose to stray from you. Help us to remember that you are still with us. Lord, hear us.

All: Lord, graciously hear us.

UNIT 2 – JESUS

ON YOUR OWN

Find somewhere quiet to do some thinking. Take a piece of paper and write 'Jesus is' at the top. Put down all your thoughts about Jesus: e.g. good, a man, etc. Keep the list handy and add more words to it during the week.

Use the Jesus Prayer: Close your eyes, and say the words 'Jesus Christ, Son of God, have mercy on me'. Repeat the words over and over in your mind, for some minutes.

RESEARCH

Learn more about Jesus this week by learning about his life and teaching from St Mark's Gospel. Read it all at once (up to chapter 11, verse 11) or read one section each day this week. Alternatively listen to a good recording of St Mark's Gospel. You may be having a quiz on this the next time you meet together.

> *Day 1:* Chapter 1 to chapter 2, verse 17.
> *Day 2:* Chapter 2, verse 18 to end of chapter 3.
> *Day 3:* Chapter 4 to chapter 5, verse 20.
> *Day 4:* Chapter 5, verse 21 to end of chapter 6.
> *Day 5:* Chapter 7 to chapter 8, verse 21.
> *Day 6:* Chapter 8, verse 22 to end of chapter 9.
> *Day 7:* Chapter 10 to chapter 11, verse 11.

WITH OTHERS – THINKING IT THROUGH

Jesus is the human face of God. He is God and he is human – this means that he was tempted as we are, but he didn't sin.

Christians believe that because human beings have chosen to disobey God's laws, they have become separated from God.

However, because God loves us, he was determined to try to rescue us, so he sent Jesus to guide us back. The plan was quite amazing! Jesus, the man who could heal the sick and restore the dead to life, willingly gave up his life and died so that the power of evil could be defeated.

God's plan means that we can find the way back to God through faith in Jesus. We can use the words of the Baptism Service (Common Worship Initiation Services):

> I turn to Christ.
> I submit to Christ.
> I come to Christ.

WITH OTHERS – GROUPWORK

Carry out as many of the group tasks as desired in order to learn more about Jesus.

Hold a quiz on St Mark's Gospel. Divide into two or more teams, allowing the members of the team to work together to answer the questions. (See the Appendix for the quiz.)

Watch a good video about the life of Jesus.

Look at the Nicene Creed in the Eucharist. In the early Church there were people who thought that Jesus was just a good man and not God, and others who thought he was God just pretending to be a man. At the Council of Nicaea in AD 325, and at a later Council, an attempt was made to write a Creed that would state Jesus was God *and* Man. Decide for yourself which phrases are put in to show that he was truly a human being and really died, and which are put in to show that he was God.

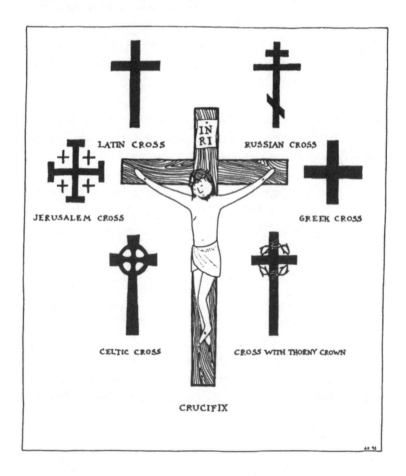

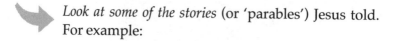

The cross is an important symbol for Christians because Jesus died for us on a cross. However, there are many kinds of crosses. Opposite are just a few. You might like to explore your church to see how many you can find and then draw the different crosses on a large sheet of paper to create a picture, using a variety of materials: e.g. pasta, cloth, wood shavings, tissue paper balls. Put the picture up in your church.

Look at some of the stories (or 'parables') Jesus told. For example:

- Matthew, chapter 13, verses 3–9 and 18–23 (the Parable of the Sower).
- Matthew, chapter 13, verses 24–30 and 36–43 (the Parable of the Weeds).
- Luke, chapter 15, verses 1–7 (the Parable of the Lost Sheep).
- Luke, chapter 15, verses 8–10 (the Parable of the Lost Coin).

What do you think these parables mean, and why does Jesus teach in this way? What do they teach you today?

Look through a hymn book used in church (either in pairs or as a group) and choose a hymn or song that speaks of our love for Jesus or his love for us. You could sing this, or perhaps the group could request that it be sung in church on the following Sunday.

Write a story or poem imagining you were a person healed by Jesus. How did you feel? How did others react?

Become journalists and investigate the death and resurrection of Jesus Christ. As a group create your own newspaper, giving eyewitness reports and pictures, and add comments by an editor on what might really have happened.

CLOSING WORSHIP

Sit or stand in a circle. The leader should read John, chapter 14, verses 1–4, and after a moment's silence the group can sing 'The Lord is my shepherd' (*Sound of Living Waters*) as a round. You may need to practise this beforehand. Alternatively sing 'Jesus is Lord', 'I am the bread of life', or 'Majesty' (all *Mission Praise*). Close by saying the Lord's Prayer.

UNIT 3 – THE HOLY SPIRIT

ON YOUR OWN

Find some time to be alone. Then hang an object like a button or a rubber from the ceiling or door-frame of your room using some cotton and a drawing pin, or Blu-Tak. Make sure that the object hangs freely. When it has stopped swinging get a chair and sit in front of your pendulum. Begin to think about what kind of things would make the pendulum move.

Finally, blow on the pendulum, making it swing. Your breath is the power that gives life to the pendulum. Can you think of anything in the world that doesn't need such a life-giving source of power to make it move or work?

Read Genesis, chapter 1, verses 1–2 and Matthew, chapter 3, verses 13–17. The Holy Spirit is thought of as the life-giving breath of God that actually made the world, and the sustaining source that gives Jesus the strength to carry out his work.

Spend a few moments thanking God for all that the Holy Spirit has given to you in your life, which enables you to grow as a Christian.

RESEARCH

Find out all you can about the wind. Look in an encyclopaedia at home, or in a library. We can't see the wind, but we can see its effect. What destructive force is it capable of? Can the wind be used in some way to work for us?

Ask two or three people in your church what they believe about the Holy Spirit. Is the Spirit as important to them as God the Creator, or Jesus Christ?

WITH OTHERS – THINKING IT THROUGH

The Holy Spirit is the power or life-giving breath of God that was present at Creation. It was the same Holy Spirit that blessed Jesus at his Baptism and gave strength and comfort to the new Church after Pentecost. It is through the Holy Spirit that God guides us in the world today.

In the Baptism Service we say that we 'believe and trust in the Holy Spirit'. It is the Holy Spirit who has helped you to grow as a Christian so that you now wish to be confirmed, and it is the Holy Spirit who will be with you on the rest of your Christian journey. Sometimes you will need support or encouragement, and the Holy Spirit will be there to give you the strength to continue.

The Holy Spirit is sometimes called the Holy Ghost, and is often portrayed as a dove, or wind, or fire in stories and pictures.

WITH OTHERS – GROUPWORK

Choose some of the following activities to continue.

Look at the results of the research carried out by the group with regard to the wind. Notice that the Holy Spirit is often referred to as 'wind' or 'breath'. Make some hand windmills, and take them outside (or blow on them) to help remember that God's life-giving power blows like the wind.

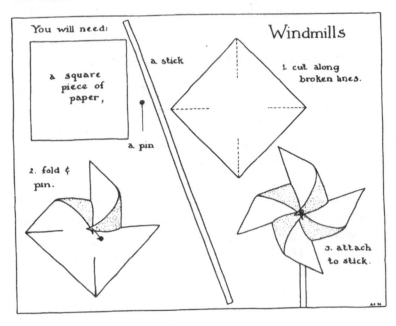

Read what happened when the Holy Spirit came to the Apostles in Acts, chapter 2, verses 1–13. Ask yourselves if we expect such things to occur today. What do the group think about faith healing or speaking in tongues, for instance? We are told that the believers met frequently for prayer in the weeks before Pentecost. Do the group think this helped?

As a group create a litany based on the Holy Spirit and wind, or the Holy Spirit and fire. Example:

Leader: Holy Spirit, your life-giving power blows stronger than the wind. Sweep through our lives and give us the desire to do your work. Spirit of power:

All: Hear our prayer.

Leader: Holy Spirit, your healing power . . .

Use the litany in church at a suitable time.

Make up some dance or movement to show the work of the Holy Spirit in the world. The song 'Spirit of the living God, fall afresh on me' (*Mission Praise*) or 'Holy Spirit, we welcome you' (*Mission Praise*) could be played while this happens. Look at different sides of the Holy Spirit – the Holy Spirit's creativity, the ability to heal, strength etc.

Look at the gifts and the fruits of the Spirit (1 Corinthians, chapter 12, verses 4–11 and Galatians, chapter 5, verses 22–26), and in twos decide what each person present possesses – what kinds of things are you good at (crafts, use of imagination, singing, keeping your temper, being happy, etc.)? Then make a large tree-trunk out of sugar paper and a number of green paper leaves and red paper fruits. Write your gifts and fruits of the Spirit on the leaves and fruit. Attach them to the tree. Display the tree in church.

Arrange to visit a service at a 'charismatic' church. Later, talk about speaking in tongues, ecstatic behaviour and faith healing. Notice that this is only one side of the Holy Spirit, who works in different ways with different people. Decide where you think the Holy Spirit is working in your church.

Cut out flame-like shapes from red, yellow or orange paper. Write prayers on them asking for the Holy Spirit's help, and hang them around the room.

Alternatively, arrange to do this in a Family Service in place of the Intercessions.

CLOSING WORSHIP

Stand in a circle and sing one of the following songs:

> 'Spirit of the living God' (*Mission Praise*)
> 'The Spirit lives to set us free' (first and last verses only) (*Songs of God's People*)
> 'Holy Spirit, we welcome you' (*Mission Praise*)

Remain standing while John, chapter 14, verses 15–17 and the Collect for Whit Sunday and / or the Post-Communion Prayer for that day (from the Common Worship Lectionary) are read. Then hold hands in the circle and say the words of the Peace used in the Eucharist to one another. (You will need to look up the words first before holding hands.) The leader could close by saying the words of the Grace.

UNIT 4 – THE TRINITY

ON YOUR OWN

 Draw a large clover leaf on a piece of paper.

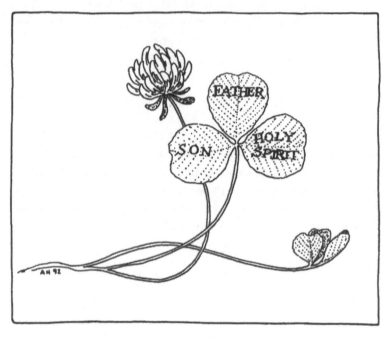

 Look at your picture and remind yourself that God is three different people, yet one person – just as the clover leaf has three parts to one leaf! So we know God as: God the Creator who made the world; God the Son who came to restore our friendship with God; and God the Holy Spirit who is the life-giving power source.

Say the words of the Grace, that great prayer to the Trinity:

May the *grace* of our Lord Jesus Christ,
and the *love* of God,
and the *fellowship* of the Holy Spirit
be with us evermore. Amen.
(Adapted from 2 Corinthians, chapter 13, verse 13)

RESEARCH

Find out all you can about the three ways that water can exist – as water, as ice, and as steam. How does this happen?

Think about yourself this week. How many different sides are there to your character? Do you behave differently at home or with friends from the way you do at school / work or church? Does this make you two (or three) different people, or simply a complex person?

Use your Bible to find three people who met God in different ways – as God the Father, as Jesus, or as the Holy Spirit. You will probably need to look in the Old Testament for the first one, and in the New Testament for the last two.

WITH OTHERS – THINKING IT THROUGH

The Trinity (the word means 'Three-in-One') is one of the greatest mysteries of our faith. Each week in the Eucharist we say in the words of the Creed that we believe in *one* God. But we then go on to say that we also believe in God the Father, God the Son and God the Holy Spirit – *one* God who is *three*!

Perhaps we shall never understand the mystery of the Trinity fully while we are in this world. After all, we the created are looking at God who made us! It may be helpful, however, to think about God as having different 'faces' or different ways of being seen. Sometimes God is experienced by people in different ways.

WITH OTHERS – GROUPWORK

Choose some of these activities to help you continue looking at the Trinity.

Draw a large symbol of the Trinity on a piece of sugar paper, and talk about God as 'Three-in-One' as you look at the symbol in front of you. What does the Trinity

CIRCLE WITHIN TRIANGLE

TRIQUETRA

TREFOIL

TRIQUETRA AND CIRCLE

mean to you? You might wish to do this in small groups of two or three. Any one of the symbols on the opposite page would be suitable.

Look at water in its three forms: as ice, water and steam. Look at all the information discovered by the group about water. Notice that water is the same in *substance* but different in *form*. Now look at the Trinity – the same in substance, but different in form!

Create some mime (in threes) to show the three different 'faces' of the Trinity. You will need to spend some time thinking about the different sides of God first!

Study John, chapter 14, verses 8–17. Jesus speaks here of God the Father, of himself, and of the Holy Spirit. Make lists of the differences between the three faces of God as shown in this reading.

Make a huge list from the Bible of people who met God. Write alongside them the way that God revealed himself to them – as God the Creator and Father, as Jesus the Son of God, or as the Holy Spirit the life-giver. Alternatively, if there are enough of you, divide into two groups, and see which group can find the most.

Get into twos and compare thoughts on the research done this week about the different sides of your character. Do you agree with each other's self-assessment? Notice how difficult it is to analyse ourselves – we who are made in the image of God. How much more difficult is it to analyse God, our Creator!

> *Study the Nicene Creed* from the Eucharist together. Look at what it says about God, Father, Son and Holy Spirit. You will probably need the help of a dictionary! List all the things you discover about God and put up the work for others to see in church.

CLOSING WORSHIP

Open this time of worship by singing 'Father God, I love you', 'Father, we adore you' or 'Holy, holy, holy is the Lord' (all *Mission Praise*). Use the images of the Trinity (the clover, pictures, or water) as a point of focus for the group. Three candles could also be lit.

The mime, or prayers of intercession, could be used; otherwise create a litany by brainstorming words on 'God the Father', 'God the Son' and 'God the Holy Spirit', as follows:

Leader: God, the Father . . .

Different group members now say any words that come into their heads about God the Father such as:

Members: Creator!
Loving!
Caring!

Leader: Hear our prayer.

(Repeat with God the Son, God the Holy Spirit, and Father, Son and Holy Spirit.)

You could close by holding hands and saying the words of the Grace.

UNIT 5 – BAPTISM

ON YOUR OWN

Spend some time on your own, thinking about what happens at a Baptism. Try to find somewhere quiet if possible, where you will not be disturbed, and when you have read through the next few instructions below, close your eyes.

Think back to the last Baptism you saw. Let your mind go back to the beginning of the service and try to imagine all that happened:

- Who was being baptized?
- Who came with them?
- What promises were made?
- What else happened in the service?

After a few moments, when you have finished thinking about the Baptism, read Acts, chapter 8, verses 26–39. The Jews thought that God's great plan was only for them, so Philip must have been very surprised that a man from Ethiopia who was not a Jew should believe in Jesus Christ and want to be baptized. Notice that there is no church building, no candles and no congregation.

RESEARCH

Find out all about your own Baptism (or someone else's, if you haven't been baptized). Where were you baptized? Who came? What did you wear? Who were your godparents or sponsors? Did you receive any special presents? Look for photographs of the occasion.

Go and see your godparents or sponsors, or write to them. What do they remember of your Baptism?

If possible, look up the entry for your Baptism in the church register and make a copy, or else find your Baptism certificate.

WITH OTHERS – THINKING IT THROUGH

In Baptism we become a member of God's Family – a follower of Jesus Christ, and so a 'Christian'. God promises to forgive us for the things we have done wrong and we are given a fresh start. We might like to think of ourselves as being washed and made clean again, or of dying and being reborn.

When a baby is baptized, godparents and parents make certain promises for them. They promise that the child will be brought up as a Christian and will return to make promises for themselves at Confirmation. Those who are baptized as adults or teenagers make these promises themselves at their Baptism and 'confirm' them again at Confirmation.

WITH OTHERS – GROUPWORK

Use as many of the tasks below as desired.

 Make a frieze out of all the Baptism material gathered by your group. Give it the heading 'Our Baptism', and place it in church.

Look at the Baptism Service used by your church.

- What promises do godparents and parents make?
- What questions are they asked, and how do they answer?
- What is the congregation's response to the Baptism?

Go into church and look at all the objects connected with a Baptism Service in your church. Discuss their use. Any of the following might be found.

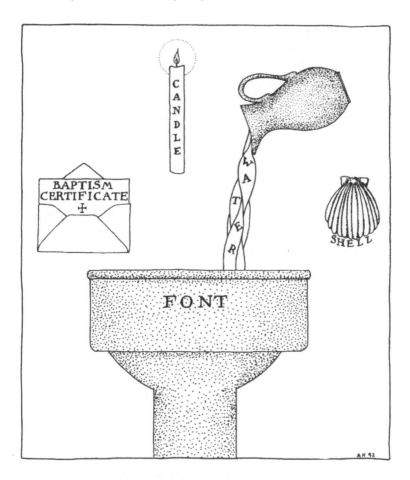

Read what happened at Jesus' Baptism in Matthew, chapter 3, verses 13–17. Talk about the subject of total immersion where the whole body is ducked under water. How do you feel about this?

Attend a Baptism Service, either of a young child or of an adult. Perhaps it might be possible to attend a service of total immersion at the local Baptist church.

Look at one of the symbols used in the Baptism Service (e.g. water or light) and brainstorm words on a piece of paper:

> *Example:* wet ... cold ... drip ...
> light ... warm ... friendly ...

Use these words to help you draw a picture or write some poetry on the theme of 'Baptism'.

Talk together about being members of the Family of God. Do the young adults in your church feel full members of the Family of Christ? If not, how can this be improved?

CLOSING WORSHIP

Sit in a circle with a lighted candle, a shell and some water in the centre. Start with a moment of silence, perhaps by using a Stilling Exercise to relax the whole body, e.g. 'Stretch your toes ... now relax ... stretch your whole foot ... now relax, etc.' It doesn't matter if eyes are open or closed.

When everyone is ready, the leader should read the words of the guided meditation in a quiet voice, allowing time for everyone to think in between the different instructions.

Guided Meditation

You are asleep . . .
your breathing is deep and even . . .
God calls you . . .
you try to ignore him . . .
but he calls again . . .
Again he calls you . . .
and you try to shrug him away . . .
once more his voice calls . . .
This time you wake up and slide out of bed . . .
Slowly you move towards the voice . . .
up the stairs . . .
getting nearer to the voice . . .
wanting to be there . . . !
At the top of the stairs there is a room . . .
the door is open and you enter . . .
Look around you . . .
It feels as though you have come home . . .
Here you are really known . . .
Here you are really loved . . .
Here God waits for you . . .
Kneel down and offer yourself to God . . .
Then after a moment leave the room aware that
you can return at any time . . . !

Quietly sing 'Father we love you' or 'Abba Father' (both
Mission Praise) and close by saying together the Collect for
the Baptism of Christ on the First Sunday of Epiphany from
the Common Worship Lectionary.

UNIT 6 – CONFIRMATION

ON YOUR OWN

Find somewhere to be quiet. Place your Baptism certificate in front of you (or a Prayer Book open at the Baptism Service) and think about why you wish to be a Christian. At your Confirmation you will publicly make for yourself the promises made for you at your Baptism. So, how important is being a Christian to you?

Take a piece of paper and a pencil and jot down all your feelings about the forthcoming Confirmation. Are you happy, nervous, worried, excited? Are you looking forward to it, or would you prefer it was all over?

Finally, offer your joys and worries to God knowing that he will be with you on this day, and end this time alone by saying the Lord's Prayer.

RESEARCH

Read through the Confirmation Service and spend time looking at promises you will be making.

Ask two different people about their Confirmation. What happened? How did they feel? Did anything special happen to them? When did they take their First Communion? Do they feel they have grown as Christians since their Confirmation, and if so, can they say in what ways?

WITH OTHERS – THINKING IT THROUGH

Confirmation is as much about God doing something as it is about us doing anything. We certainly 'confirm' (or agree) that we wish to be Christians, publicly in front of a lot of people. But God is doing something too. He confirms his blessing upon us that he first gave at our Baptism.

Confirmation is often a kind of 'passing-out parade' for young Christians, a time when they leave the Church, instead of being the start of a new period in their Christian life. It is important to remind yourself that Confirmation is the beginning of a new life, and not the end of it.

Like all new lives, it may not be easy. You may find it difficult to keep the wonderful promises you made at your Confirmation. But remember, it's hard to remain on the mountain-top all the time! Most of life is lived down in the boredom of the valley!

You may find it hard to fit in with the other full members of the church, or you may feel that some of the church worship isn't for you. But as with all changes in your life (for instance, moving to a new house) remember that it's worth persevering and taking things slowly, one step at a time.

WITH OTHERS – GROUPWORK

Use some of the following suggestions.

Together, look at the results of your questions to other Christians about their Confirmation, and at members' feelings about their own approaching Confirmation.

Explore 'Keeping my word' with other group members. Make a frieze on 'Failing to keep my word', and apply headlines, either made-up or cut from newspapers. Continue by discussing promises the group have broken. How did they feel? Were they forgiven?

Then look again at the promises that will be made at Confirmation. Remember these too will be broken, because we are human! But God is always ready to forgive us. Starting again is a *daily* task!

 Use a candle as a focal point and sit round it in a circle.

Think about the phrase 'I turn to Christ'. What does it mean? Put down any thoughts on a piece of paper. If there is time, do the same with the other two promises made at the Confirmation Service: 'I repent of my sins' and 'I renounce evil'. Cut out all the words and stick them on a sheet of paper. Put the results up in church.

Look at the custom of Confession and discuss it with your parish priest. Some people may wish to make their Confession before their Confirmation.

Find out more about the diocese in which you live, and make a collage about it to place in church. As a full member of the church you will also be a member of the wider Anglican Church. Can you find out anything about this?

Go on retreat with all the members of the Confirmation group, perhaps for 24 hours or a weekend, to help prepare yourselves for the Confirmation.

Rehearse the Confirmation Service. Where will you sit, and what will happen? Practise going forward to kneel before the Bishop.

Make a Rule of Life. Your new life will be different from the old one. As a group, or alone, decide upon some rules for this new life. Use the following headings:

> Worship.
> Prayer.
> Giving.
> Concern for others.

Make a copy of your Rule of Life and hand it to your minister. Look at this again in a year's time. Will you manage to keep to the Rule?

CLOSING WORSHIP

Use some candles and a jug of water as focal points. Start with a moment's silence, then say the Lord's Prayer together. Read Ezekiel, chapter 36, verses 25a and 26–28.

Then take the jug of water and, using a bowl and a towel, rinse the hands of each person (or use the water to sign a cross on each person's forehead), inviting them to say the following words:

> Lord, you wash me clean from my sins. Help me to start a fresh life.

Close by using the words of St Francis of Assisi: 'Lord, make us instruments of your peace' (page 120, Common Worship Initiation Services) and sing 'Seek ye first' (*Mission Praise*) if desired.

UNIT 7 – THE BIBLE

ON YOUR OWN

Make a special place in your bedroom, or somewhere else in the house, to read your Bible. This could be a chair with a small table or ledge beside it on which to base the Bible. You prop the Bible up, use a special bookmark, or make a cover for it out of wallpaper or spare material. Try to make this area peaceful – a place where you can read the Bible or think about God.

Try to read a few verses of the Bible every day. Use a daily Bible-reading scheme like the Bible Reading Fellowship's *Daylight*. Or choose a special book in the Bible to read. You may like to start with the Acts of the Apostles. Read only a small amount at first, and don't worry if you miss a day, simply pick up your Bible and start again.

Hold your Bible in your hands and think about God. Ask God to help you understand what he is saying to you.

RESEARCH

Find out how many different versions of the Bible there have been. For example, there is the Good News Bible and the Revised Standard Version, but how many others are there? What languages was the Bible first written in? Ask other Christians, or at your local library.

Look at a Bible story you know well in two different translations of the Bible, e.g. Genesis, chapter 1, verses 1–5 (the creation of the world) or Luke, chapter 2, verses 1–7 (the birth of Jesus). Are they different? Is one easier to understand? Decide which you prefer.

Alternatively, ask some Muslim friends about their religious book, the Koran. What is it about? Where do they keep the Koran?

If you have some Jewish friends, perhaps they too can tell you more about their scriptures.

WITH OTHERS – THINKING IT THROUGH

Our Bible tells us about God's great love for the whole of creation. We see God's great plans for the earth – how human beings can be reconciled again, after choosing to go their own way.

In the Old Testament we see the first part of God's plan. He forms a special relationship with a small nation, Israel, and makes an agreement (or 'covenant') with them that they will be his people and he will be their God. Again and again they break this agreement, but always God forgives them.

In the New Testament the second part of God's plan begins. The Messiah, Jesus the Son of God, is born into a family belonging to the House of David. Through him God's great act of love will be completed, and people will be reconciled once more to God.

WITH OTHERS – GROUPWORK

Use as many of the following ideas as you wish.

Look at how many versions of the Bible were found. When were they translated? Which do you prefer and why? Draw a huge chart, showing all the Bibles you have managed to find, in date order.

Find out how many books there are in the Bible itself. Can you list all these books and say to which of the following categories you think each belongs:

> history; biography; letters; songs; prophecy; law; poetry; stories.

You might like to find examples in the Bible itself of poetry, history, etc. Photocopy them and create a large frieze to show the range of different styles used in the Bible. Put it up in church to help others to learn more about the Bible.

Arrange a visit to a cathedral, abbey or museum, to find out how Bibles were written and illustrated by hand in medieval times. Then make your own examples of illuminated writing.

Find out more about the meaning of 'covenant'. Look at the covenants made with Noah (Genesis, chapter 9, verses 1–17), Abraham (Genesis, chapter 15, verses 13–21), and Moses (Exodus, chapter 6, verses 2–8). Then look at the New Covenant which Jesus made (Jeremiah, chapter 31, verses 31–34; Mark, chapter 14, verse 24; and 1 Corinthians, chapter 11, verse 25). We make covenants today (e.g. Baptism and Marriage); are they easy to keep? Should we be forgiven if we break them?

Look at a number of Bible-reading schemes. Decide which you like. Buy one and start reading. Or arrange for the whole group to write their own Bible-reading scheme. Get reading!

Play some music while everyone sits quietly reading their Bibles.

Study a passage of the Bible together. What does God have to say to you today?

Listen to a tape or record of some of the Psalms, sung by a choir. Make some 'emotion' pictures to show how you feel while you are listening to the music: paint anything you like to express how you feel, but all in different shades of *one* colour.

Read from the Dramatized Bible (HarperCollins 1989). Allocate parts and read one or two passages from the Bible. Or do some drama or mime based on a Bible story.

CLOSING WORSHIP

Place a Bible on a low table with candles on both sides. Be silent for a moment and allow yourself to think of all that you have learnt about God's word. Then say the words of the Collect for the Last Sunday after Trinity (Common Worship Lectionary). Sing 'Rejoice in the Lord always' or 'Seek ye first' (both *Mission Praise*), and close by reading verse 105 of Psalm 119.

UNIT 8 – PRAYER

ON YOUR OWN

 Find some time to be alone, then ask yourself this question:

 In silence think about all the different ways you can communicate with God: talking, listening and silence are just a few ways. Are there others?

Finally say the Lord's Prayer slowly, stopping at the end of each line. Try to think about each section.

RESEARCH

Carry out a study into the prayer habits of two or three people. Be careful that you don't terrify them! Ask the following questions:

1. Do you think prayer is important? *Yes/No.*
2. Do you pray regularly or occasionally? *Regularly/ Occasionally.*
3a. If you pray regularly, when is that? *Morning/ Afternoon/Evening.*
  b. If you pray occasionally, when is that? *Morning/ Afternoon/Evening.*
4. Do you use a Prayer Calendar, or set prayers? *Yes/No.*
5. How much of your prayer time is about yourself? *All/Two-thirds/Half /Third.*
6. Do you ever say 'arrow' (or emergency) prayers? *Yes/No.*
7. Do you say Grace at meals? *Yes/No.*
8. Do you teach your children to pray? (adults only) *Yes/No.*
9. How much listening do you do in your prayers? *Half/Third/Quarter of prayer time/None.*
10. How often do you forget to pray? *Never/Occasionally/Frequently.*

Many churches use Prayer Calendars to help them pray for different people. Find out if your church has a Calendar of Intercessions (that is, 'prayers for other people') or a Prayer Board or Book.

WITH OTHERS – THINKING IT THROUGH

Prayer is the way we communicate with God. Just as we may pick up a telephone to speak to a friend or write them a letter, with God we open our hearts and minds in prayer. As with the times when we speak with friends, our talk with God is also two-way, although God may not answer us directly or in the way we expect. Prayer is *listening* to God as well as *speaking*.

Like other forms of communication, prayer needs to be practised. It's not something we only do on Sunday at church. Hopefully, it will become as normal as breathing in or out, and a part of our whole life.

WITH OTHERS – GROUPWORK

Use as many of the groupwork exercises as will be helpful.

Try spending some time in silent prayer or meditation. At first do this for only three or four minutes. Make yourself comfortable, and use something to act as a focal point: an icon, flowers, or a cross. Think of a subject like 'God' or 'the world', and simply offer your thoughts to God. Try to allow some space for silence in your head – God can't communicate with you if you talk too much! Discuss the experience with other group members and your leader.

Collect a number of local and national newspapers. Find things to pray about, cutting out any suitable stories or pictures and making them into a frieze. Use the ideas to make up simple one-line prayers.

> *Make prayer books.* Copy out favourite prayers into an exercise book and make up new prayers. Stick in photographs and pictures and prayer biddings. Make a note of what you have prayed for, and the date. Don't forget to add the result later!

> *Look at some well-known prayers* from the Prayer Book. Look up, and read, the following well-known prayers:

- The General Confession.
- The Prayer of Humble Access from the Eucharist.
- The Post-Communion Prayer for the Sunday Next before Advent (Common Worship Lectionary).
- The Eucharistic Prayer.
- The Third Collect for Evensong.

> *Make up some mime or movement,* in groups of three or four, to go with the words of the Lord's Prayer. When you feel happy with the movement, try it out while one person reads the words aloud. This could be offered in church next week.

> *Look at the research gathered* about the prayer habits of the congregation, and decide when and where you will say your prayers. Make written covenants or promises to God about your prayer time. Offer these during worship and perhaps remake them each year on the anniversary of your Confirmation.

> *Make up a plan* of the prayers you wish to say *before* going to a Communion Service. Think about those leading and attending the service, as well as yourself.

Try using a number of different prayer positions. When would you wish to use any of them? For example:

- Standing.
- Sitting.
- Kneeling.
- Eyes open/eyes closed.
- Head bent/head up.
- Lying down.
- Arms raised.
- Hands raised.

 Hold a prayer vigil the evening before the Confirmation. Make out a rota so that everyone spends half an hour in church in prayer. You could ask other members of the congregation to join you, and make prayer cards for use at the vigil.

CLOSING WORSHIP

Give each member of the group a small candle in a holder. Light the candles and stand in a circle facing each other. Sing 'O Lord hear my prayer' (Taizé) a number of times and then place the candles together in the centre of the circle, perhaps on a small table. Sit down.

The leader should introduce a number of 'biddings' (or subjects) and allow group members to add a few words. Keep them short and simple! Each person ends with 'Lord, hear us', and all reply, 'Lord, graciously hear us'. Close by holding hands and singing the calypso version of the Lord's Prayer.

Alternatively the group could write down their own confessions and take them outside and burn them in a suitable container. Sing the Russian Orthodox version of 'Kyrie eleison' (*Songs of God's People* or *Songs and Prayers from Taizé*).

UNIT 9 – THE CHURCH

ON YOUR OWN

Find two pictures or photographs, one of a church building and one of a group of people of all ages. Spend some moments looking at them. Remind yourself Jesus' Church is made up of *people*. It is not just a building!

Take a piece of paper and a pencil, and draw a line down the page. Write 'Church' on one side and 'Christian' on the other. Brainstorm any words that come into your mind under either heading. When you've finished, look at the two lists. Are they the same or different?

Put the pictures and the brainstorm paper on the floor in front of you. Then offer your Church – its people and ministers – to God. Thank God for all they have done in the past and for all they do now.

RESEARCH

Find out all you can about the history of your parish church.

Discover more about the Parochial Church Council and the Deanery Synod. If possible, attend one of these as an observer.

WITH OTHERS – THINKING IT THROUGH

The Church is made up of people. We might think of the people as a 'Family of God'. The Christian message belongs to this whole family, and not just to individuals. Therefore it's almost impossible to be a Christian and not meet together with other Christians.

Christianity is about sharing and being with others, not about taking or getting what you want. So to moan about worship as being 'boring' or complain that you get nothing out of it makes no sense. Christians meet together to encourage and help each other – to give and not to take, although in giving we often receive help ourselves.

The Church of God also meets for other reasons: to say sorry, to give thanks, to learn, to be refreshed, and to ask for help. At Confirmation we become full members of the Church, responsible for the Christian health of others as well as our own.

WITH OTHERS – GROUPWORK

Use some of the suggestions to explore this theme further.

Look at the results of the brainstorm on the words 'Church' and 'Christian'. Are there any surprises? Do the lists look the same? Can anything be learnt from this?

Make a display of all the information gathered about your parish church, and if possible arrange to have a guided tour of the building where you meet each week. Look at the font, the altar and the pulpit as you hear about the history of the church.

Read the story of the new Church in Acts, chapter 1, verses 12–26; chapter 2, verses 40–47; and chapter 4, verses 32–37. Is this anything like the Church that you know today?

Take a walk around the parish and explore its boundaries. Find out how many people live in your parish and how many come to church. Are there other churches in the parish? If so, are their services different? Do they ever get together? Is there an ecumenical church in the area, and if so, what is special about it? Make a map of the parish, showing where the churches are, and where most of your church family live.

Go to another church to experience their worship. Invite a minister or member of that church to join you and ask them questions. Be careful that your questions don't cause offence.

Ask the Parish Priest or Curate to talk about the vestments (or special clothes) that he or she wears for different services. Perhaps you can try some on. Find out about the different clothes worn by a Reader, a Deacon and a Bishop, and talk about 'the ordained ministry'. Also look at the vessels used for the Communion Service and find out their names.

Ask your Parish Priest to tell you more about his or her job. What do they do all week, and can they think of ways in which you can help them?

Find out about all the jobs that have to be done in the Church and create a display about them. Talk to as many people as possible about their work for the Church. Read 1 Corinthians, chapter 12, verses 4–11. Do you have any people doing these jobs in your church?

Ask a Churchwarden to speak to you about their job. They are responsible for much of the running of the church. How can you help?

CLOSING WORSHIP

If possible focus on an icon, and possibly burn some incense. Particularly do this if icons and incense are not normally used in your church. After a moment's silence read John, chapter 15, verses 12–17. Then say the words of welcome in the Baptism Service to remind yourselves that you are all members of God's Family. Close by quietly singing 'I will enter his gates with thanksgiving in my heart' (*Mission Praise*).

UNIT 10 – THE EUCHARIST

ON YOUR OWN

Take a piece of paper and a pencil and find somewhere quiet to sit. Think about the times when your family or friends get together. What family customs do you have? For instance, at Christmas do you hang up stockings or decorate the tree together? Are there other times in the year when you have special ways of doing things in your family?

> *Read the story* of the Last Supper as told by St Paul in 1 Corinthians, chapter 11, verses 23–26. We remember this event each week at the Eucharist (or Communion Service).

> *Thank God* for the special things you do together with family and friends, and for the special service of the Eucharist when Christians meet together to remember that Jesus gave his life for them.

RESEARCH

Look up the following reading and work out what *objects* have become important to Christians as a result of the action it describes:

Matthew, chapter 26, verses 17–29.

Ask two or three people who attend church regularly the following questions:

1. What are the most important *objects* in a church building for you?
2. If you could have one thing to remind you of God, what would it be?

WITH OTHERS – THINKING IT THROUGH

Our lives are full of important symbols – that is, actions and objects that remind us of something else. For instance, a ring on the third finger of the hand may just be a ring, but it can also be a symbol of love and marriage.

For Christians there are two special services, given to us by Jesus, which are full of symbolic action: the Eucharist and Baptism. They are called *sacraments*. God uses a simple action, like eating a meal, to remind us that Jesus gave his body and blood for us so that we could be reunited with God. The eating of the meal is also a sign of an internal change that takes place inside us when we receive the bread and wine in faith. By sharing in the eucharistic meal we are strengthened spiritually and leave the church better able to cope with the next day.

WITH OTHERS – GROUPWORK

Use some of the suggestions below.

 Look at the different ways that families celebrate Easter or Christmas. What other special rituals do your family have, not connected with a Christian festival? Which of these are important to you?

Walk round your church building. Which parts are special to you? What are your earliest memories of church and worship? As a group look at the answers to your research about people's favourite *objects* in church. Make a report on your findings and present it to the PCC or congregation.

Look up the other five sacramental rites used in church in the Prayer Books:

- Confirmation.
- Marriage.
- Ordination (service at which men and women are made deacons or priests).

- Absolution (the proclaiming of forgiveness of sins).
- Unction (the placing of holy oil on the forehead of someone, often when ill).

Can you work out together what are the outward signs (or symbolic actions) of what is received inwardly?

 Hold an Agapé. 'Agapé' is the Greek word for the love that friends have for one another, and to Christians an Agapé is a special 'friendship meal' where people show that they care for one another. Encourage everyone to be involved in planning and preparing the meal: where it will be eaten, who will act as hosts, what food will be eaten. Then choose some special readings from the Bible or other suitable book and read these before and during your meal.

Act out the story of the Last Supper. Read the story through and then try pretending you were there. Make up your own words. Afterwards talk about what it felt like to be the different 'actors' during that meal.

Hold a Passover meal at Easter. For information on how to hold a Christian Passover meal use *Passover Seder for Christian Families* by Sam Mackintosh (published by Resource Publications Inc.) or *The Sermon Slot (Year 1)* by S. Swain (published by SPCK).

Practise how to receive the Communion bread and wine.

Look at some of the different names for the Eucharist:

- *The Eucharist* (which means Thanksgiving).
- *The Mass* (taken from the closing words of the old Latin Service when the people were dismissed to share in God's work).
- *The Communion Service* (we are together in communion with God and each other).
- *The Lord's Supper* (remembers the Last Supper).

Decide which of these titles you prefer, and why.

Attend a Eucharist and then look at the words in the Prayer Books. Imagine the service as a meal – the host welcomes the guests; they remember past stories; the food is prepared and brought in; the people eat together; the host says goodbye to the guests.

Help to prepare a Eucharist where all ages will be worshipping. Look particularly at the readings, sermon, and intercessions. How can you help keep young children interested as well as adults of all ages? What are the difficulties and how will you solve them?

CLOSING WORSHIP

Place a plate of bread and a glass of wine on a small table. The group might like to sit round this in a circle. Sing one of the following songs (all from *Mission Praise*):

> 'I am the bread of life'
> 'Jesus stand among us'
> 'Let us break bread together'

Read 1 Corinthians, chapter 11, verses 23–26. Hold up the bread and the wine when they are mentioned in the reading. End by saying together the words of the prayer Agnus Dei (i.e. 'Jesus, Lamb of God') from the Prayer Book.

UNIT 11 – THE CHURCH'S YEAR

ON YOUR OWN

 Think about the different seasons and holidays of an ordinary year. Make a list of them, starting with Christmas. What's next? Continue through the year to the next Christmas.

Look at old photographs, or a video, that remind you of your favourite time of the year.

Thank God for the different seasons, festivals, and holidays of the year. Pray for people who can't enjoy them.

RESEARCH

Using the list you made of the seasons of the year, find out the seasons of the Church's Year, and add these. Look in the Prayer Books!

Ask at least five Christians for their favourite time of the Church's Year.

WITH OTHERS – THINKING IT THROUGH

The Church's Year begins in Advent. This might seem an odd time to start a new year, but other people start them at odd times. The school year starts in September, the financial year in April, and the Chinese New Year in February!

Another good reason for starting the year before Christmas is to allow us to prepare for Christmas. The time of Advent and the time of Lent which comes before Easter are great times of thinking and preparation. After these solemn times come the great festivals of Christmas and Easter.

You might think the most important festival of the year for Christians is Christmas, but in fact Easter is the major festival. Christians are Easter people – they are brought to life again, just like Jesus!

WITH OTHERS – GROUPWORK

Carry out some of the following assignments.

Look at the calendars made by everyone, and make a complete calendar of the Church's Year – large enough to put up in church.

Look at favourite seasons of the year and decide as a group your favourite time of the Church's Year.

Look at the preparations carried out at home for Christmas. Do you think we should also prepare ourselves spiritually? If so, make an Advent calendar and write 24 tasks behind the 'doors' to help you prepare yourself for Christmas. Use this next Advent.

Make a large collage to show some of the Lent and Easter practices carried out in Christian churches. You might like to find out more about: Pancake Day celebrations; Mardi Gras; ashing; well dressing; the giving of flowers on Mothering Sunday; Palm Sunday processions with donkeys and palms; and Easter gardens.

Go through the Church's Year and look up the readings in the Lectionary of readings for each event. Notice that the Common Worship Lectionary has a three-year cycle of readings. Find out whether you are in year A, B or C.

Think up some imaginative Lenten promises. Is it helpful to give up things like sweets or is it better to promise to do something, like visiting an elderly person?

Finally, make a Lenten promise and write it down. See if the whole group could attend the Ash Wednesday service together and offer their written promises. Redeem these (claim them back) on Easter Day during the service.

 Invite a member of the Orthodox or Roman Catholic Church to join you and discuss their Easter ceremonies.

Listen to some music written for a church festival: the Easter anthems; the Advent antiphons; or the Litany as used at Advent or Easter.

Make up a dance suitable for Easter or Good Friday.

CLOSING WORSHIP

Gather in a circle. Put a seasonal object at the centre of the circle: e.g. twigs, flowers, dead leaves, a cross, manger, or picture of a dove. Read something appropriate to the season, and sing a well-known seasonal hymn. Say the Grace together.

UNIT 12 – THE PRAYER BOOKS

ON YOUR OWN

 Spend some time this week getting to know the Book of Common Prayer or the services replacing the Alternative Service Book. If you don't have copies, ask the Parish Priest if you can borrow them. Start by finding and reading the Confession in the Service of Morning Prayer.

Find out which week of the Church's Year you are in and prepare for Sunday worship by looking at the readings.

Use the Collect (prayer) for the week each day as part of your quiet time.

RESEARCH

Look up the following things until you feel able to find services easily:

- The Communion Service.
- The Psalms.
- Morning Prayer.
- The Baptism Service.
- The Confirmation Service.
- Evening Prayer.

Find and read the following:

- The Third Collect during Evening Prayer.
- The General Thanksgiving.
- The Ten Commandments.
- The instructions before the Communion Service.

Ask five members of the congregation which they prefer – the older or newer services – and why.

WITH OTHERS – THINKING IT THROUGH

As you will have discovered, the Church of England has one Prayer Book – the Book of Common Prayer (BCP for short) – and modern alternatives for most services.

Most of the worship in an Anglican church will be found in these books, although there are some other prayers and services allowed by bishops in their dioceses. Because we are the 'established', or official Church in England, we use the services agreed by the General Synod of the Church of England and by Parliament.

Churches may use either the BCP or the modern equivalent as authorized by the Church and Parliament. So, for instance, a couple getting married may choose the Marriage Service from the BCP rather than its modern equivalent. Or a Communion Service early on a Sunday morning may be from the BCP, but later in the day a Family Communion Service might be a modern form of worship.

WITH OTHERS – GROUPWORK

Choose some tasks from the following.

Go to some different services at your church. Use the appropriate service book and try to follow the worship.

 Look at the Marriage Service in both traditional and modern forms, especially at the reasons why couples should get married. Which service do members of the group prefer, and why?

Challenge one another to see how quickly you can find your way around the books. For example, find:

1. The Creed.
2. Psalm 119.
3. The Baptism Service for adults.

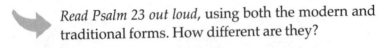 *Read Psalm 23 out loud*, using both the modern and traditional forms. How different are they?

Look up the readings for the day, and read them aloud.

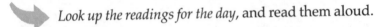 *Find out about the history* of the Book of Common Prayer. How did it come to be written, and why?

Make up a display of different prayer books of all sizes and shapes, and place it in church. Note who they were given to and when. Be sure you can return them to their owners afterwards.

Interview some of the congregation and ask them which are their favourite prayers or passages in the prayer books. Create a display in church out of their answers.

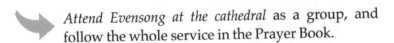 *Attend Evensong at the cathedral* as a group, and follow the whole service in the Prayer Book.

CLOSING WORSHIP

Close by saying the service of Evening Prayer. The leader should make any explanations regarding the service beforehand, for example:

- Psalms will be read alternately: everyone reads the opening verse, and then each side takes alternate verses, with everyone saying the Gloria.
- Sit for readings, but stand for the Psalms and Canticles (which should be said).
- Canticles will be read together.

UNIT 13 – CHRISTIAN WITNESSES

ON YOUR OWN

Find somewhere quiet and let your mind go back to your earliest memories. Who were the most important adults in your life? It might have been Mum or Dad, or your grandparents, or someone else. Have you one really good memory of an adult who made you feel loved or special?

Now try to think of one Christian today who is very special to you. It might be someone you know locally, or someone famous.

Thank God for the adults who loved and cared for you when you were small, and for the example of Christians alive today.

RESEARCH

Go to the library and find out about the life of a famous Christian.

Look in the Prayer Book or Lectionary for the names of major saints remembered in church. What saints are remembered this month? Have they been mentioned in worship or have you held a special service to remember them? Not every church will have done this.

October

1	
2	
3	
4	*Francis, Friar, c.1226*
5	*William Tyndale, Translator of the Bible, 1536*
6	
7	
8	
9	
10	*Paulinus, Bishop, Missionary, 644*
11	
12	
13	*Edward the Confessor, King of England, 1066*
14	
15	*Teresa of Avila, Mystic, 1582*
16	
17	
18	*St. Luke the Evangelist*
19	
20	

WITH OTHERS – THINKING IT THROUGH

All Christians are called to be saints, but there have always been those who were considered especially holy. By their life and behaviour they have taught others to love God.

The first such people to be called saints were of course the eleven Apostles. Notice that Judas Iscariot did not become a saint!

Gradually, other special Christians were included: Mary, the mother of Jesus; Saul of Tarsus who became Paul; and many others who were killed because of their beliefs.

Many of our churches are named after saints, and people use their names in prayer. The example they gave us of how to be a Christian never fades. Indeed we speak of Christians who are dead as still being part of the Church of God – after all, they are alive with God! Since the Reformation the Church of England has not created new saints (although the Roman Catholic and Orthodox Churches still do), but has chosen special people to be remembered and celebrated on certain days.

WITH OTHERS – GROUPWORK

Choose some of the tasks below.

Look at all the memories you have uncovered this week of people who loved and helped you when you were young. Discuss them with each other.

Find out about the history of your church. Is it dedicated to a saint, and if so, what can you find out about them? Does your church have a special saint's chapel or statues of different saints? Or perhaps there are special people connected with your church who, though not saints, set a good example to others. Ask the oldest members of the congregation about special Christians who might have been alive when they were younger.

Visit your local cathedral. What saint(s) is it dedicated to? Look for chapels dedicated to saints, or a shrine covering the bones of a saint. The early history of the cathedral may be connected with one or more saints.

Talk about the kind of person a saint should be. Should they be perfect or are they allowed to make some mistakes? Who do you think would make a good saint today?

Make up some drama on the life of a local saint and perform this in church at a suitable time.

Find out about saints who have the same names as members of the group or their families.

Make up a saints game by making pairs of cards with a saint's name on them. Turn them face-down and take it in turns to guess where the matching pair lie.

Make 'stained glass' windows out of tissue paper and card (or sugar paper), showing the picture of a saint. Photocopy a picture of a saint and enlarge it until the lines of the drawing become thick. Lay this on black sugar paper or thin card and hold it down. Use a craft knife to cut round all the black lines of the picture. Either cut through the sugar paper or card or apply enough pressure to mark it and cut through this afterwards. Stick small pieces of coloured tissue paper over the picture as desired to make the coloured-glass effect.

Investigate the different emblems and colours for saints. Give everyone a saint's name and the task of finding out about their particular saint. Call each other by the new names.

CLOSING WORSHIP

Use a picture of a saint (or an icon or some of the stained glass windows) as a focal point and sit in a circle. Material from the *Cloud of Witnesses* (Collins, 1982) could be read if there is a saint's day approaching. Or read aloud some information found about any saint. Finally ask for God's help to follow the good example of his saints. Close by singing the first verse of 'For all the saints'.

UNIT 14 – STEWARDSHIP

ON YOUR OWN

 Take a piece of paper and list all the ways you have been cared for since you were a baby. For example, you have been clothed, fed, given a home, etc. Add to the list over the next few days as you think of other things.

Imagine that you have been given £1 million to spend on helping others. How would you spend it? Make a detailed plan of how you could best use the money to help as many people as possible.

Read the Parable of the Three Servants in Matthew, chapter 25, verses 14–30.

RESEARCH

Find out whether your church has a stewardship plan to help people plan their giving to the church. This could be an envelope scheme for giving money regularly, or it might be a way of organizing how time and talents are used to help the church.

Ask your Church Treasurer how much it costs to finance your church each year.

WITH OTHERS – THINKING IT THROUGH

All that the Christian possesses belongs to God. Our world, our life, our good health, our talents (whether it's being good at English, painting or mechanics), our money and even our time, all belong to God because he has given them to us.

We are given all these things to be 'stewards' of them – that is, to look after them and use them to continue God's work in the world. We might think of ourselves as the managers of a business who have to do the best job possible with the materials and staff given to us. If the business isn't successful the owner will want to know why we have wasted his money.

How we care for our world and the way that we live our life is important, for God gives us the opportunity of sharing in his work, if we will!

WITH OTHERS – GROUPWORK

Choose some of the tasks set out below.

Look at the lists made this last week of everything your family has given to you. How can you thank them for all that they do or have done? Come up with a list of different ways you could show your gratitude. Can you put any of them into operation immediately? Offer prayers for your family.

How did you decide to spend £1 million on other people? Decide *as a group* what one thing you would like to give to the people in your area.

Invite some members of the church to speak to you about the needs of the church. You could ask people from:

- The choir.
- Servers.
- Mission or pastoral work.
- Children's work.
- Churchyard maintenance.

Think about offering your time, your talents or your money to help one of these groups. You might, for instance, wish to join the choir or help cut the grass in the churchyard.

Think about making a promise to dedicate some of your gifts towards God's work in the world. Write these down and offer them at a service in church before your Confirmation Service or at your closing group worship.

Covenant Form

I promise with God's help to:

....

....

....

Signed...

Date...

As a group carry out a community project connected with the environment. Any of the following would be suitable:

- Clear out a ditch or pond, or an area of waste ground.
- Have a litter-clearing day in your area.
- Start a collection of recyclable materials.
- Tidy up your churchyard.
- Hold a story afternoon for pre-school children and their parents, and read to them a number of 'green' stories.

Look carefully at the talents of everyone in the group, and then see if you can help with a Family Service. Could you do some drama, or a dramatized reading? You will need to speak to your Parish Priest.

Invite the Treasurer to speak about the church's finances. Talk about how much money you might be able to give on a regular basis.

Paint a large picture on the theme of 'Christian Stewardship', and place the completed work in church.

Look up the following Bible readings and talk about the idea of 'service'. Jesus was called to be the 'servant of all', and we are called to serve others. What do you feel about this, and what form might your service take?

- Matthew, chapter 20, verses 25–28.
- Luke, chapter 22, verses 25–27.
- Philippians, chapter 2 , verses 5–8.
- 2 Corinthians, chapter 4, verse 5.
- Matthew, chapter 5, verses 14–16.

The Church's mission is to bring people to God. Discuss how you as a member of the Church might do this. Could you become involved in any parish mission work?

CLOSING WORSHIP

In silence place a candle on a table or stand and light it. Allow the group to watch the flame for a moment, then place a hollow tube over the candle so that the flame cannot be seen.

Read Luke, chapter 11, verses 33–36 and then uncover the flame. Sing either 'We really want to thank you, Lord', 'Make me a channel of your peace' or 'Spirit of the Living God' (all *Mission Praise*), and use the Collect for the Second Sunday after Trinity (Common Worship Lectionary). Close by shaking hands with each other and saying 'May the Light of Christ be with you'.

UNIT 15 – THE CHRISTIAN LIFE

ON YOUR OWN

Take a large piece of paper and on it brainstorm examples about good and evil in the world. For example you might put 'Hospitals' down for good, or 'War' for evil. Add to your ideas throughout the week.

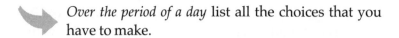 *Over the period of a day* list all the choices that you have to make.

Ask God's help to make the right choices each day this week, and spend some moments before you go to bed asking his forgiveness for the times you chose wrongly. Remember you're not alone – the Holy Spirit is there to guide and help you!

RESEARCH

Using newspapers and magazines gather stories about people who have to make choices or decisions.

Look up stories about the following people in the Bible. What choices did they have to make?

- Noah (Genesis, chapter 6).
- Joseph (Matthew, chapter 1).
- Abraham (Genesis, chapters 12 and 22).
- Ruth (Ruth, chapter 1).
- Hannah (1 Samuel, chapter 1).
- Levi (Mark, chapter 2).
- Jesus (Matthew, chapter 4, and Luke, chapter 22).
- Peter (Mark, chapter 14).

WITH OTHERS – THINKING IT THROUGH

Every day we have to make choices – about what we do and think. Sometimes this is easy and at other times harder. Sometimes the decision isn't very important, but at other times it may be a decision that will change our whole life.

As Christians we choose to follow Jesus and his ways, but we live in a world that prefers to ignore him. Often the ways of the world are completely opposite to God's. So every single day of our life we are forced to choose between God's way and the world's way. Every day we can be tempted to choose wrongly.

If the Christian life sounds impossible, we must remember that God knows that we are weak. No matter how many times we get it wrong, God offers to forgive us, if we are sorry. So each day we can start afresh, trying again to get it right!

Being a Christian doesn't mean we are good people (rather the opposite, really), but it does mean we know we need God's help to get it right. So God gives us his Church to be with others – helping each other to live the Christian life – and he gives us the Holy Spirit to enable us to make the right choices and stick to them.

WITH OTHERS – GROUPWORK

Choose some of the activities below to look at your Christian life.

Produce some drama to show the power of good and evil in the world. Use any of the following as a starting point:

- A family argument over 'skiving off work'.
- Wanting to go to athletics on a Sunday morning instead of church.
- A powerful leader.

Look at the choices that members of the group have had to make in the previous week. Encourage everyone to be honest and to keep information private within the group. Which choices were difficult? Which were wrong?

Look up the Ten Commandments (Exodus, chapter 20, verses 1–17) and the two great commandments given by Jesus (Mark, chapter 12, verses 28–31). Which of these commandments do you think we break most often? Create prayers of confession based on them. Make them into a book or use them in church.

Invite a speaker to talk about drugs, AIDS or sex, and think about 'making Christian choices' with regard to these subjects.

Role-play the following ethical story:
You are the Governors of a large Christian charity raising money for projects in Third World countries. Recently your income has gone down and you have had less to spend on others. However, your manager has now come to you with a suggestion. He thinks you should put all your money into the tobacco (or drink) industry on the Stock Exchange for one year. During that year you will not be able to help new projects, but at the end of the year you will have made an enormous profit which can then all be sent to Third World countries.

Give out different parts and think up some emergency projects that need money now, e.g. food for starving people in Africa, clean water projects in India. Look at whether you should place charity money on the Stock Exchange (it's a bit like gambling) and whether you should place the money into the tobacco or drink industry (do you want to encourage people to drink or smoke?).

Don't worry if you can't come up with a solution. Life is full of such dilemmas!

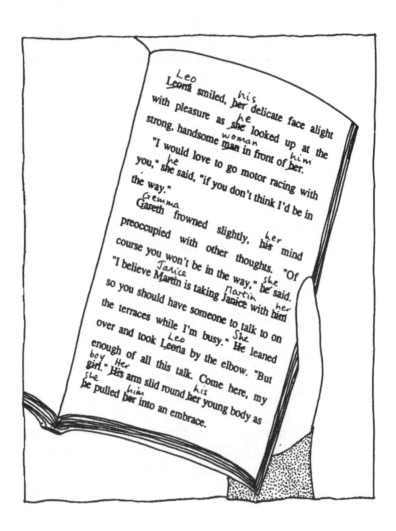

Read a book or magazine story together, changing all the male and female roles. A love story would be particularly suitable. Every time the word 'he' appears, change it to 'she'. Do the same for 'him', 'she' and 'her' and change the people's names as well.

After the reading, talk about the subject of 'sexism'. Does it exist in our society and if so, does it matter? Can, and should, men and women be equal? Should couples both go out to work when they have children? Should child-minders be used? Alternatively look at the subject of ageism, instead of sexism.

Role-play being a Christian in a non-Christian family. How will your life differ from the rest of the family? Try to keep the Christian as 'normal' as possible, and don't become too 'goody-goody'!

Plan a week's shopping for a family, buying foods which won't harm the environment, and not supporting countries which have poor civil rights records. You will need to do some research to find out which foods can be bought, and come to a decision between you about which products, companies, and countries you wish to support. Finally, make a display to be placed in church to encourage others to buy responsibly.

Find out about Traidcraft, and organize an exhibition of its work in your church.

Look up 1 Corinthians, chapter 13. Study this passage. What do you think is 'true love'?

CLOSING WORSHIP

Hold hands and sing 'Father God, we worship you' or 'Bind us together, Lord' (both *Mission Praise*). You may need to write the words down so that everyone can see them. Spend a few moments in silence thinking of the mistakes that you have made this week. Then in turn encourage everyone to say 'I . . . (name) repent of my sins'. The rest of the group should answer 'May the Father, Son and Holy Spirit forgive you'. Close by saying the Lord's Prayer.

Appendix

Quiz on the Life and Teaching of Jesus
(based on St Mark's Gospel)

1. What was the name of the man whose daughter was brought to life? (Jairus: chapter 5, verses 21–43.)
2. Name the twelve Apostles. (Simon Peter, James and John, Andrew, Philip, Bartholomew, Matthew, Thomas, James son of Alphaeus, Thaddaeus, Simon the Patriot and Judas Iscariot: chapter 3, verses 16–19.)
3. How many people did Jesus give bread to? (5,000 and 4,000 people: chapter 6, verses 30–44 and chapter 8, verses 1–10.)
4. What did James and John ask Jesus? (Whether they could sit at the right and left hand of Jesus when he ascended his throne: chapter 10, verses 35–45.)
5. What was the name of the blind man who shouted loudly to Jesus to have pity on him? (Bartimaeus: chapter 10, verses 46–52.)
6. What did Jesus say to the little children? ('Come to me, because the kingdom of heaven belongs to such as these . . .': chapter 10, verses 13–16.)
7. Who baptized the people? (John the Baptist: chapter 1, verses 4–5.)
8. Which of Jesus' disciples were fishermen? (Simon, Andrew, James and John: chapter 1, verses 14–20.)
9. Who was Levi? (The tax collector: chapter 2, verse 14.)
10. What is the Parable of the Mustard Seed? (The kingdom of heaven is like the smallest seed in the world which becomes the biggest of plants: chapter 4, verses 30–32.)

11. Who is the greatest? (A child: chapter 9, verses 33–37.)
12. Who baptized Jesus? (John the Baptist: chapter 1, verses 9–11.)
13. What happened when Jesus was asleep in a boat? (A storm came up, the disciples were afraid, and Jesus calmed the storm: chapter 4, verses 35–41.)
14. What happened to Simon's mother-in-law? (She was ill and Jesus healed her: chapter 1, verses 29–31.)
15. What happened to Jesus in Nazareth? (They rejected him and he was unable to do any miracles there: chapter 6, verses 1–6.)
16. How did John the Baptist die? (Herodias' daughter asked for John the Baptist's head to be cut off: chapter 6, verses 14–29.)
17. What happened at the Transfiguration? (Jesus and three disciples went up a mountain. Jesus' clothing became white and he was seen talking to Moses and Elijah: chapter 9, verses 2–13.)
18. What did Jesus ride into Jerusalem? (A colt/donkey: chapter 11, verses 1–10.)
19. What was the name of a group of people who criticized Jesus? (Pharisees: e.g. chapter 8, verses 11–12.)
20. What happened to the woman who touched Jesus' cloak? (She was healed of severe bleeding: chapter 5, verses 25–34.)